Writer's Workbook

Level 1

Blackline Masters

A Division of The McGraw-Hill Companies

Columbus, Ohio

www.sra4kids.com

SRA/McGraw-Hill

A Division of The McGraw·Hill Companies

Send all inquiries to:
SRA/McGraw-Hill
8787 Orion Place
Columbus, OH 43240-4027

Printed in the United States of America

ISBN 0-07-569559-6

1 2 3 4 5 6 7 8 9 QPD 06 05 04 03 02 01

Table of Contents

Unit 6   Journeys

Expository Writing

Unit 7   Keep Trying

Narrative Writing

Unit 8   Games

Descriptive Writing

Unit 9   Being Afraid
Poetry

Unit 10   Homes
Persuasive Writing

Cumulative Checklists

▶Autobiography

 Plan

Draw pictures about you.
Write words about you.

1. _____

- - - - - - - - - - - - - - -

2. _____

- - - - - - - - - - - - - - -

3. _____

- - - - - - - - - - - - - - -

4. _____

- - - - - - - - - - - - - - -

Objective: Students plan to write about themselves by drawing pictures and words.

Copyright © SRA/McGraw-Hill. Permission is granted to reproduce this page for classroom use.

▶ **Autobiography**

Plan

Make a web about you. Each circle should be something different about you. Use your web ideas.

THE WRITING PROCESS

Write

Write a story about you.

▶**Autobiography**

Revise

Read your autobiography. Make changes to make it better. Think about these things.

Ideas

☐ Do you want to add an idea?

☐ Do you want to take out an idea?

Order

☐ Is there a better order for your ideas?

Word Choice

☐ Are there better words to use about you?

Proofreading Marks

∧	Add something.
—	Take out something.
≡	Make a capital letter.
⊙	Add a period.

Objective: Students read what they wrote about themselves and make changes to make it better.

▶**Autobiography**

THE WRITING PROCESS

Check

Read your autobiography. Check for these things.

Capital Letters

☐ at the beginning of a sentence

☐ for names of people

☐ for names of cities and states

☐ for the word *I*

End Marks

☐ period, question mark, or exclamation point at the end of a sentence

Spelling

☐ of all your words

Share

Copy your autobiography and get ready to read it out loud. Draw a picture to go with it.

▶ Writing a List

Write a list of things you would need
to take when you visit someone.
Write a title for your list.

▶ **Writing a Shopping List**

Write a list of things you buy at the grocery store.

_____

- -

_____

_____

- -

_____

_____

- -

_____

_____

- -

_____

_____

- -

_____

PERSONAL WRITING

▶Writing a Numbered List

Write a list to tell what you do before
you go to school.

What I Do Before I Go to School

_____

- -

_____

- -

_____

- -

_____

- -

_____

- -

_____

- -

_____

Objective: Students write a numbered list.

▶ Writing a List for Another Person

Write a list of things a person needs to bring for a camping trip. Write a title for your list.

_____

_ _ _ _ _ _ _ _ _ _ _ _ _ _ _ _ _ _ _ _

_____

_____

_ _ _ _ _ _ _ _ _ _ _ _ _ _ _ _ _ _ _ _

_____

_____

_ _ _ _ _ _ _ _ _ _ _ _ _ _ _ _ _ _ _ _

_____

_____

_ _ _ _ _ _ _ _ _ _ _ _ _ _ _ _ _ _ _ _

_____

_____

_ _ _ _ _ _ _ _ _ _ _ _ _ _ _ _ _ _ _ _

_____

PERSONAL WRITING

Name _____ Date _____

▶Writing a Journal

Write your journal page.

_____

- -

_____

_____

- -

_____

_____

- -

_____

_____

- -

_____

_____

- -

_____

_____

- -

_____

Objective: Students write a journal entry.

Copyright © SRA/McGraw-Hill. Permission is granted to reproduce this page for classroom use.

Name _____ Date _____

▶Writing a Journal

Write about your favorite animal and how it moves.

_____

- -

_____

- -

_____

_____

- -

_____

_____

- -

_____

_____

- -

_____

_____

- -

_____

_____

- -

_____

PERSONAL WRITING

▶Writing a List in a Journal

Write a list of things that have wheels.

_____

– –

_____

_____

– –

_____

_____

– –

_____

_____

– –

_____

– –

_____

_____

– –

_____

_____

– –

_____

Objective: Students write a list as a journal entry.

UNIT 3 Things That Go • **Lesson 10** *On the Go*

▶ Journal Pictures

Draw a picture of something that goes.

_____

- -

_____

Write words or a sentence about your picture.

_____

- -

_____

- -

_____

- -

PERSONAL WRITING

Name _____ Date _____

▶Learning Log

Objective: Students begin a learning log.

Draw a picture. Complete the sentences.

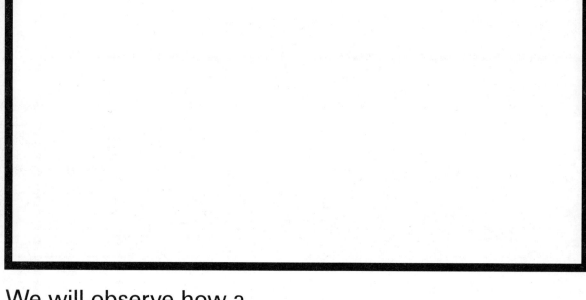

We will observe how a

_____

– – – – – – – – – – – – – – – – – – – –

_____ moves on

_____

– –

_____

_____

– –

and _____ .

Personal Writing • **Writer's Workbook**

UNIT 3 **Things That Go • Lesson 13** *Trucks*

▶**Learning Log**

PERSONAL WRITING

Write a learning log of your observation.

_____

— — — — — — — —

Day _____

Write two sentences to tell what happened.

_____

— — — — — — — — — — — — — — — — —

_____

— — — — — — — — — — — — — — — — —

_____

— — — — — — — — — — — — — — — — —

_____

— — — — — — — — — — — — — — — — —

_____

UNIT 3 Things That Go • **Lesson 14** *Trucks*

▶**Learning Log**

Objective: Students continue a learning log by recording observations.

Write your learning log.

_____

\- \- \- \- \- \- \- \- \-

Day _____

Tell what happened in order.

_____

1. _____

2. _____

3. _____

4. _____

Copyright © SRA/McGraw-Hill. Permission is granted to reproduce this page for classroom use.

Personal Writing • **Writer's Workbook**

▶**Learning Log**

Draw a picture to show how the object moved on one surface. Tell about your picture.

_____

- - - - - - - - -

Day _____

PERSONAL WRITING

_____

_____

_____

_____

_____

_____

▶Invitation

Plan

Who will get your invitation?

☐ a family member

☐ a teacher

☐ a friend

_____

– – – – – – – – – – – – – – – – – –

☐ other _____

Why are you writing an invitation?

☐ to invite someone to a party

☐ to invite someone to a school event

_____

– – – – – – – – – – – – – – – – – –

☐ other _____

_____

– – – – – – – – – – – – – – – – – –

_____

Objective: Students plan for an invitation by writing the audience and purpose.

Copyright © SRA/McGraw-Hill. Permission is granted to reproduce this page for classroom use.

Name _____ Date _____

▶ **Invitation**

Answer these questions to help plan
your invitation.

My Invitation

_____

- -

Who is invited? _____

_____

- -

What is the event? _____

_____

- -

What day is it? _____

_____

- -

What time is it? _____

_____

- -

Where is it? _____

_____

- -

Who is giving the event? _____

Write your invitation on a sheet of paper.

PERSONAL WRITING

Objective: Students revise an invitation by adding, rearranging, or changing.

▶ **Invitation**

Revise

Read your invitation. Use this checklist to make your invitation better. Use these marks to make changes.

Ideas

☐ Do you want to add something to the invitation?

☐ Did you write everything the reader needs to know?

Order

☐ Did you write the information in order?

☐ Did you write your name at the end?

Word Choice

☐ Are there better words to use in your invitation?

Proofreading Marks

∧	Add something.
—	Take out something.
≡	Make a capital letter.
⊙	Add a period.

Copyright © SRA/McGraw-Hill. Permission is granted to reproduce this page for classroom use.

► **Invitation**

Check

Read your invitation. Use this list to make sure you remember to check everything.

☐ Did you leave spaces between the words?

Capital Letters

☐ Did you begin the person's name with a capital letter?

☐ Did you begin your sentence with a capital letter?

☐ Did you begin the weekday and month with a capital letter?

Spelling

☐ Did you spell your words correctly?

Share

☐ Copy your invitation onto a clean sheet of paper.

☐ Use your best handwriting.

☐ Address the envelope. Put a stamp on the envelope.

PERSONAL WRITING

▶Thank-You Note

Plan

Whom do you want to thank?

☐ a teacher

☐ a family member

☐ a friend
_____

- -

☐ other _____

Why are you writing a thank-you note?

☐ someone gave you a gift

☐ someone helped you

☐ someone did something kind
_____

- -

☐ other _____

_____

- -

_____

Objective: Students generate ideas for a thank-you note.

▶**Thank-You Note**

PERSONAL WRITING

 **Plan**

Plan what you want to say in your thank-you note. Write your ideas.

1. Tell what the person did for you or gave to you.

_____

_ _ _ _ _ _ _ _ _ _ _ _ _ _ _ _ _ _

_____

_ _ _ _ _ _ _ _ _ _ _ _ _ _ _ _ _ _

_____

2. Tell why it was important to you.

_____

_ _ _ _ _ _ _ _ _ _ _ _ _ _ _ _ _ _

_____

_ _ _ _ _ _ _ _ _ _ _ _ _ _ _ _ _ _

_____

 **Write**

Write your thank-you note. Write your ideas in sentences. Add a greeting and closing.

Revise

▶ **Thank-You Note**

Read your note. Use the checklist to make your note better. Use these marks to make changes.

Proofreading Marks

∧	Add something.
—	Take out something.
≡	Make a capital letter.
⊙	Add a period.

Ideas

☐ Is your note written to a specific person?

☐ Does your note thank the person for a specific gift or something he or she did?

Order

☐ Would your sentences make more sense in another order?

☐ Did you start your note with *Thank you?*

☐ Did you end your note with a closing?

Word Choice

☐ Are there other words you can use to tell how you feel?

Sentence Fluency

☐ Does each sentence add a new thought to your note?

☐ Are there sentences that you want to take out?

Thank-You Note • **Writer's Workbook**

Name _____ Date _____

▶ **Thank-You Note**

Check

Use this list to make sure you remember to check everything.

☐ Did you start at the left and go to the right?

Capital Letters

☐ Check the beginning of each sentence.

☐ Check the beginning of all names.

☐ Check the word **I**.

End Marks

☐ Check for the correct end mark for every sentence.

Spelling

☐ Check the person's name.

☐ Check all of the words.

Share

☐ Make a card or copy your note onto a clean sheet of paper. Use your best handwriting.

PERSONAL WRITING

UNIT 4 Our Neighborhood at Work • **Lesson 12** *Worksong*

▶ Friendly Letter

Plan

Who is going to read your friendly letter?

☐ a grandparent

☐ a family member

☐ a teacher

☐ a friend

☐ other _____

Why are you writing a friendly letter?

☐ to tell about something you did

☐ to tell about somewhere you went

☐ to tell about something that happened

☐ other _____

_____

Friendly Letter • **Writer's Workbook**

UNIT 4 Our Neighborhood at Work • **Lesson 12** *Worksong*

▶**Friendly Letter**

Plan the message of your friendly
letter. Write your ideas.

_____

- -

First _____

_____

- -

Next _____

_____

- -

Last _____

Write

Write each idea in a sentence. Add a
greeting and closing.

PERSONAL WRITING

▶**Friendly Letter**

Revise

Read your letter. Use this checklist to make your letter better. Use these marks to make changes.

Proofreading Marks

∧	Add something.
—	Take out something.
≡	Make a capital letter.
⊙	Add a period.

Ideas

☐ Does your letter tell something that is interesting to your reader?

☐ Does each sentence tell something new?

Order

☐ Are your sentences in an order that makes sense?

☐ Did you begin your letter with a greeting?

☐ Did you end with a closing?

Word Choice

☐ Are there words you can add to tell more details?

Sentence Fluency

☐ Do your sentences sound good, one after the other?

Objective: Students revise a friendly letter by adding, deleting, changing, or rearranging.

Copyright © SRA/McGraw-Hill. Permission is granted to reproduce this page for classroom use.

UNIT 4 Our Neighborhood at Work • **Lesson 15** *Unit Wrap-up*

▶**Friendly Letter**

Check

Use this list to make sure you remember to check everything.

☐ Are there spaces between your words?

Capital Letters

☐ Does every sentence begin with a capital letter?

☐ Do names begin with capital letters?

☐ Is the word **I** a capital letter?

End Marks

☐ Does evey sentence have an end mark?

Spelling

☐ Did you spell your words correctly?

Share

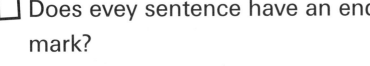

☐ Copy your letter neatly onto a clean sheet of paper.

☐ Draw a picture.

☐ Address an envelope. Put a stamp on the envelope. Mail your letter.

PERSONAL WRITING

▶ Writing Instructions

Plan

Who will read your instructions?

☐ your teacher

☐ your family

_____

- - - - - - - - - - - - - - - - -

☐ other _____

Why are you writing instructions?

☐ to tell how to get ready for a kind of
weather

_____

- - - - - - - - - - - - - - - - -

☐ other _____

Write the idea you are going to use to write your instructions.

_____

- - - - - - - - - - - - - - - - -

_____

_____

- - - - - - - - - - - - - - - - -

 **Writing Instructions**

EXPOSITORY WRITING

Plan

Plan your ideas below.

First

Next

Then

Last

 Write

Write your sentences on a sheet of paper.

▶ **Writing Instructions**

Revise

Use this checklist to make your instructions better. Use proofreading marks.

Proofreading Marks

∧	Add something.
—	Take out something.
≡	Make a capital letter.
⊙	Add a period.

Ideas

☐ Did you write all of the steps?

☐ Are there any ideas you want to add or take out?

Order

☐ Would your sentences make more sense in another order?

Word Choice

☐ Are there other words you can use to make the instructions clearer?

☐ Did you use order words?

Sentence Fluency

☐ Does each sentence tell the reader exactly what to do next?

Make any changes on your paper.

Objective: Students revise their writing by adding, deleting, changing, or rearranging.

Copyright © SRA/McGraw-Hill. Permission is granted to reproduce this page for classroom use.

▶ **Writing Instructions**

Check

☐ Did you write a title?

☐ Did you write adjectives in your instructions?

Capital Letters and End Marks

☐ Did you begin your sentences with a capital letter and use end marks?

Spelling

☐ Did you spell your words correctly?

Share

☐ Draw a picture of each step on a clean sheet of paper.

☐ Copy each sentence neatly under the correct picture.

☐ Glue your picture and sentence papers to poster board.

☐ Write your title at the top of the poster board.

☐ Use your poster to explain what to do.

EXPOSITORY WRITING

Signs

Who will look at your sign?

☐ your classmates

☐ your teacher

☐ visitors to your class

_____

- -

☐ other _____

Why are you making a sign?

☐ to tell where to put things in the
   classroom

_____

- -

☐ other _____

Write the idea you will use for your sign.

_____

- -

_____

_____

- -

_____

UNIT 5 Weather • **Lesson 7** *How's the Weather?*

▶**Signs**

EXPOSITORY WRITING

Write

Make a sign. Use your ideas to write words and draw pictures.

Revise

Use this checklist to make your sign better. Use proofreading marks to make changes.

Ideas

☐ Do your words and pictures go together?

Word Choice

☐ Are there words you can add to tell more?

☐ Are there different words you can use?

Make any changes on your paper.

Proofreading Marks

∧	Add something.
—	Take out something.
≡	Make a capital letter.
⊙	Add a period.

▶**Signs**

Check

A sign must have a clear message so that the readers will know what they need to know. Use this list to make sure you remember to check everything.

☐ Did you draw a picture for your sign?

☐ Did you spell your words correctly?

☐ Are there spaces between your words?

Share

Use the checklist to get your sign ready to share.

☐ Copy your sign neatly onto a clean sheet of paper. Use your best handwriting.

☐ Draw the picture neatly on the paper.

☐ Color the picture.

☐ Glue your sign to a piece of poster board.

☐ Ask your teacher to hang up your sign in the classroom.

▶Writing Labels

Write the name of a kind of weather on the line. Draw a picture of that kind of weather. Write a label for all the parts of your picture.

_____

- - - - - - - - - - - - - - - - - - - -

_____

EXPOSITORY WRITING

▶Writing a Summary

Objective: Students generate ideas for a summary.

Plan

Who is going to read your summary?

☐ your teacher

☐ your family

☐ your class

_____

- -

☐ other _____

Why are you writing a summary?

☐ to tell about a story I have read

_____

- -

☐ other

Write the title and author of the story.

_____

- -

_____

_____

- -

_____

Copyright © SRA/McGraw-Hill. Permission is granted to reproduce this page for classroom use.

Name _____ Date _____

▶**Writing a Summary**

EXPOSITORY WRITING

Plan your summary. Make a box for
the beginning, the middle, and the
end. Write a label in each box. Write
words or a sentence in each box.

Beginning

Middle

End

Write

Write your sentences on a sheet of
paper.

Objective: Students revise their writing by adding, deleting, changing, or rearranging.

▶ Writing a Summary

Revise

Use this checklist to make your sentences better. Use proofreading marks to make any changes.

Ideas

☐ Did you write about the beginning, middle, and end?

☐ Did you write at least one detail about the story?

☐ Do you want to take out any ideas?

Order

☐ Do your sentences tell the order of the story?

Word Choice

☐ Are there other words you can use to tell more about the story?

Sentence Fluency

☐ Does each sentence tell something different about the story?

Make any changes on your paper.

Proofreading Marks

∧	Add something.
—	Take out something.
≡	Make a capital letter.
⊙	Add a period.

▶ **Writing a Summary**

Check

☐ Did you write the title of the story?

☐ Did you write the author of the story?

Capital Letters

☐ Did you begin every sentence with a capital letter?

☐ Did you use capital letters for the author's name?

End Marks

☐ Did you write an end mark at the end of every sentence?

Spelling

☐ Did you spell your words correctly?

Share

☐ Copy your summary neatly onto a clean sheet of paper.

☐ Draw a picture that shows what you wrote in your summary.

☐ Read your summary aloud to your class.

EXPOSITORY WRITING

Objective: Students generate ideas for a book report.

▶Writing a Book Report

Plan

Who is going to read your book report?

☐ your teacher

☐ your class

☐ a friend

_____

– – – – – – – – – – – – – – – – – – – –

☐ other _____

Why are you writing a book report?

☐ to tell about the main character in a book

☐ to tell about the events in a book

_____

– – – – – – – – – – – – – – – – – – – –

☐ other _____

Write the title of the book.

_____

– – – – – – – – – – – – – – – – – – – –

_____

Copyright © SRA/McGraw-Hill. Permission is granted to reproduce this page for classroom use.

▶**Writing a Book Report**

EXPOSITORY WRITING

Plan

Use the web to plan your book report. Write the name of the character in the middle circle. Then write one idea that tells how the character looked, felt, or acted in each of the outer circles.

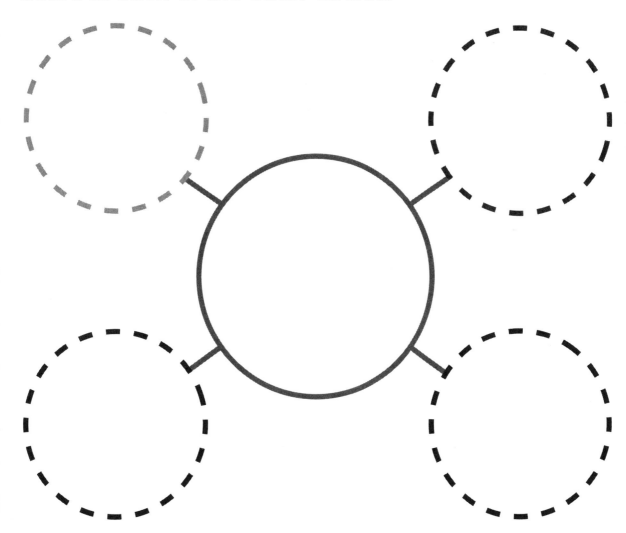

Write

Write your sentences on a sheet of paper.

Objective: Students revise their writing by adding, deleting, changing, or rearranging.

▶ Writing a Book Report

Revise

Use this checklist to make your book report better. Use proofreading marks to make any changes.

Proofreading Marks

∧	Add something.
—	Take out something.
≡	Make a capital letter.
⊙	Add a period.

Ideas

☐ Do you tell about what happened in the book?

☐ Do you tell enough about the main character?

Order

☐ Would your sentences make more sense in another order?

Word Choice

☐ Are there other words you can use to tell more about the character?

Sentence Fluency

☐ Does each sentence tell something different about the main character?

☐ Are there sentences you can take out?

Make any changes on your paper.

Copyright © SRA/McGraw-Hill. Permission is granted to reproduce this page for classroom use.

▶ **Writing a Book Report**

Check

☐ Did you write the title of the book?

☐ Did you write the author of the book?

Capital Letters

☐ Did you begin each sentence with a capital letter?

☐ Did you begin names with capital letters?

End Marks

☐ Did you write the correct end mark after every sentence?

Spelling

☐ Are words spelled correctly?

Share

☐ Copy your book report neatly onto a clean sheet of paper.

☐ Draw a picture of the main character in the book.

☐ Read your book report to your class.

EXPOSITORY WRITING

Objective: Students generate ideas for writing directions.

Copyright © SRA/McGraw-Hill. Permission is granted to reproduce this page for classroom use.

▶**Writing Directions**

Plan

Who will read your directions?

☐ your classmates

☐ a visitor

_____

- -

☐ other _____

Why are you writing directions?

☐ To tell how to go from the classroom
to another place in the school

_____

- -

☐ Other _____

I am going to write directions to tell
someone how to go from

_____

- -

_____

- -

to _____ .

Name _____ Date _____

UNIT 6 Journeys • **Lesson 7** *Me on the Map*

▶**Writing Directions**

Plan

Plan your directions.

1.

2.

3.

4.

Write

Write your sentences. Use your plan.

Objective: Students revise their writing by adding, deleting, changing, or rearranging.

► **Writing Directions**

Revise

Use this checklist to make your directions better.

Ideas

☐ Do your directions tell how to go from your classroom to another place?

☐ Do you need to add any steps?

☐ Do you need to take out any steps?

☐ Does your map go with your directions?

Order

☐ Are your sentences in order?

Word Choice

☐ Did you write position words?

Sentence Fluency

☐ Does each sentence tell about one step?

Make changes on your paper.

Proofreading Marks

∧	Add something.
—	Take out something.
≡	Make a capital letter.
⊙	Add a period.

UNIT 6 Journeys • **Lesson 10** *Me On the Map*

► **Writing Directions**

EXPOSITORY WRITING

Check

☐ Are there spaces between the words?

☐ Does your writing go from left to right?

Capital Letters and End Marks

☐ Do all sentences begin with a capital letter and end with an end mark?

Spelling

☐ Did you spell the words correctly?

Share

☐ Copy your directions neatly onto a clean sheet of paper.

☐ Copy your map neatly onto a clean sheet of paper.

☐ Trade directions with a classmate. Read and follow each other's directions.

▶Writing a Report

Plan

Who is going to read your report?

☐ your teacher

☐ your class

☐ your family

☐ another class

_____

- - - - - - - - - - - - - - - - - - - -

☐ other _____

Why are you writing a report?

☐ to write about a national landmark

_____

- - - - - - - - - - - - - - - - - - - -

☐ other _____

I am going to write a report about

_____

- - - - - - - - - - - - - - - - - - - -

_____

UNIT 6 Journeys • **Lesson 12** *The Library Trip*

▶ **Writing a Report**

Plan

Use the web to plan your report. Write the topic in the middle circle. Write a different idea in each of the outer circles.

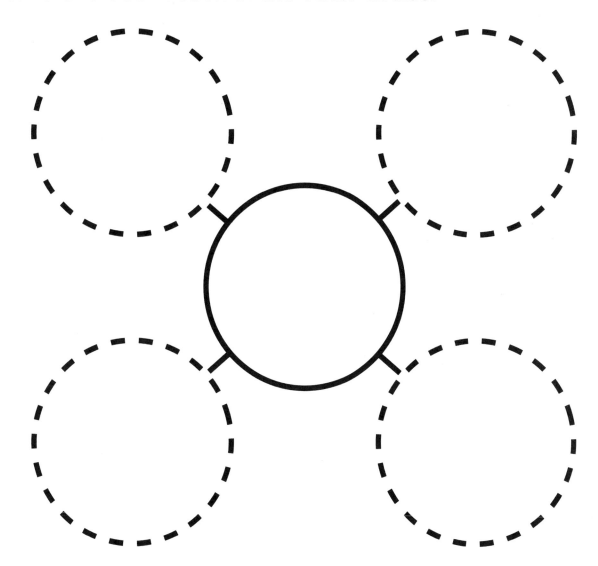

EXPOSITORY WRITING

Write

Write sentences for your report on a sheet of paper.

Objective: Students revise their writing by adding, deleting, changing, or rearranging.

► **Writing a Report**

Revise

Ideas

☐ Did you write only facts about your topic?

☐ Do your sentences tell enough about the topic?

Order

☐ Does your first sentence tell the topic of your report?

☐ Does your last sentence tell about your first sentence?

☐ Do all of your sentences tell about the topic?

Word Choice and Sentence Fluency

☐ Are there other words you can use to tell more about each fact?

☐ Does each sentence tell a different fact about the topic?

Make any changes on your report.

Proofreading Marks

∧	Add something.
—	Take out something.
≡	Make a capital letter.
⊙	Add a period.

▶ **Writing a Report**

Check

☐ Did you write a title?

Capital Letters

☐ Did you begin names of people and places with capital letters?

☐ Did you begin every sentence with a capital letter?

End Marks

☐ Did you write an end mark after every sentence?

Spelling

☐ Did you spell the words correctly?

Share

☐ Copy your report neatly on a clean sheet of paper.

☐ Draw a picture of the topic of your report.

☐ Read your report aloud to your class.

EXPOSITORY WRITING

▶A Story About Me

Objective: Students write the audience and purpose for a story about themselves.

Plan

Who is going to read your story?

☐ a teacher

☐ a parent

☐ your class

☐ a friend

_____

- -

☐ other _____

Why are you writing a story about you?

☐ to tell about something I tried to do

☐ to tell about something that
    happened to me

_____

- -

☐ other _____

_____

- -

▶**A Story About Me**

NARRATIVE WRITING

 **Plan**

Use a story map to plan your writing.
Write ideas about what you will put in
each part of your story.

Beginning

Middle

End

Write

Use your story map to write a story
about yourself.

Objective: Students make a plan for writing a story.

Copyright © SRA/McGraw-Hill. Permission is granted to reproduce this page for classroom use.

▶**A Story About Me**

Objective: Students revise writing by adding, deleting, rearranging, or changing.

Revise

Read your story. Use the checklist to make your sentences better. Use these marks to make changes.

Proofreading Marks

∧	Add something.
—	Take out something.
≡	Make a capital letter.
⊙	Add a period.

Ideas

☐ Do you want to add any ideas?

☐ Does each sentence tell something different?

☐ Did you write a title for your story?

Order

☐ Did you write the problem at the beginning?

☐ Did you tell the things you tried in order?

☐ Did you write how the problem was solved at the end?

Word Choice

☐ Are there other words you can use to tell more?

Sentence Fluency

☐ Do your sentences sound like they go together?

►**A Story About Me**

Check

Use this list to help you remember to check everything.

Capital Letters

☐ Did you begin every sentence with a capital letter?

☐ Did you write the word I with a capital letter?

End Marks

☐ Did you write the correct end mark at the end of every sentence?

Spelling

☐ Did you spell your words correctly?

Share

☐ Copy your writing neatly onto a clean sheet of paper. Use your best handwriting.

☐ Draw a picture of yourself.

☐ Trade your story with a classmate. Read each other's story.

NARRATIVE WRITING

▶A Story About Someone You Know

Objective: Students make a plan for writing a story.

Plan

Who is going to read your story?

☐ a teacher

☐ a family member

☐ a friend

☐ the person in your story

_____

- - - - - - - - - - - - - - - - - -

☐ other _____

Why are you writing this story?

☐ someone helped you do something

☐ someone helped you learn
something

☐ someone helped you make
something

_____

- - - - - - - - - - - - - - - - - -

☐ other _____

UNIT 7 Keep Trying • **Lesson 3** *The Kite*

▶**A Story About Someone You Know**

Plan

Use a story map to plan your writing.
Write ideas for what you will put in
each part of the story.

Beginning

Middle

End

Write

Use your story map to write your story.

NARRATIVE WRITING

Objective: Students revise their writing by adding, deleting, rearranging, or changing.

UNIT 7 Keep Trying • **Lesson 3** *The Kite*

▶**A Story About Someone You Know**

Revise

Read your story. Use the checklist to make your story better.

Proofreading Marks

∧	Add something.
—	Take out something.
≡	Make a capital letter.
⊙	Add a period.

Ideas

☐ Did you use all the ideas from your story map?

☐ Did you tell enough about how the person helped you?

☐ Did you write a title for your story?

Order

☐ Did you write the problem in the beginning?

☐ Did you tell things in the order they happened?

☐ Did you write an end to your story?

Word Choice

☐ Did you use the exact words you wanted?

Sentence Fluency

☐ Do your sentences go together?

Copyright © SRA/McGraw-Hill. Permission is granted to reproduce this page for classroom use.

UNIT 7 Keep Trying • **Lesson 3** *The Kite*

▶**A Story About Someone You Know**

Check

Use this list to help you remember to check everything.

Capital letters

☐ Do names begin with a capital letter?

☐ Did you write the word **I** with a capital letter?

End Marks

☐ Did you write an end mark at the end of every sentence?

Spelling

☐ Did you spell your words correctly?

Share

☐ Copy your story neatly onto a clean sheet of paper. Use your best handwriting.

☐ Draw a picture of you and the person who helped you.

☐ Read your story to three of your friends.

NARRATIVE WRITING

UNIT 7 Keep Trying • **Lesson 4** *The Garden*

▶ Picture Book

Who is going to look at your picture book?

☐ a younger person

☐ a family member

☐ a grandparent

☐ a teacher

☐ a friend

☐ other _____

Why are you writing a picture book?

☐ to tell about something I learned to do

☐ to tell about something I learned

☐ other _____

Objective: Students make a plan for making a picture book.

Name _____ Date _____

 Picture Book

Plan

Use the sequence map to plan your picture book.

First	Next

Then	Last

Write

Use your sequence map to make a picture book.

NARRATIVE WRITING

UNIT 7 Keep Trying • **Lesson 4** *The Garden*

▶**Picture Book**

Revise

Look at your pictures. Read your sentences. Use this checklist to make your picture book better.

Ideas

☐ Did you draw a picture for each part of your story?

☐ Did you tell about each step?

Order

☐ Did you write your sentences in the correct order?

☐ Would your sentences make more sense in another order?

Word Choice

☐ Are there other words you could use to tell how you felt in each picture?

Sentence Fluency

☐ Do your sentences go together?

Proofreading Marks

∧	Add something.
—	Take out something.
≡	Make a capital letter.
⊙	Add a period.

Objective: Students revise their writing by adding, deleting, rearranging, or changing.

UNIT 7 Keep Trying • **Lesson 4** *The Garden*

▶ **Picture Book**

Check

Use this list to help you remember
to check everything.

Spacing

☐ Are there spaces between words?

Capital Letters

☐ Did you begin each sentence with a capital
letter?

End Marks

☐ Does every sentence have an end mark?

Spelling

☐ Did you spell your words correctly?

Share

☐ Copy each sentence neatly onto a clean
sheet of paper.

☐ Draw a picture above each sentence.

☐ Make a front and back cover for your book.

☐ Put your pages in order between the covers.

TIVE WRITING

▶Make-Believe Story

Objective: Students make a plan for writing a story.

Plan

Who is going to read your make-believe story?

☐ your class

☐ a teacher

☐ a family member

☐ a friend

☐ other _____

- - - - - - - - - - - - - - - - - -

_____

Why are you writing this story?

☐ to tell about someone or something that keeps trying to do something

_____

- - - - - - - - - - - - - - - - - -

☐ other _____

_____

- - - - - - - - - - - - - - - - - -

_____

Name _____ Date _____

▶**Make-Believe Story**

NARRATIVE WRITING

Plan

Use a story map to plan your make-believe story.

Characters	Beginning

Middle	End

Write

Use your story map to write a make-believe story.

UNIT 7 Keep Trying • **Lesson 6** *The Fox and the Grapes*

▶ **Make-Believe Story**

Revise

Read your sentences. Use this checklist to make your story better. Use these marks to make changes.

Objective: Students revise their writing by adding, deleting, rearranging, or changing.

Proofreading Marks

∧	Add something.
—	Take out something.
≡	Make a capital letter.
⊙	Add a period.

Ideas

☐ Did you write a title?

☐ Are there any ideas you want to add to your story?

☐ Is it clear that your story is make-believe?

Order

☐ Does your story have a beginning, middle, and end?

☐ Did you write your sentences in an order that makes sense?

Word Choice

☐ Are there words you can add to tell more about your character?

Sentence Fluency

☐ Do your sentences go together?

UNIT 7 Keep Trying • **Lesson 6** *The Fox and the Grapes*

▶ **Make-Believe Story**

Check

Use this list to help you remember to check everything.

Direction

☐ Did you start at the top and write to the bottom?

☐ Did you start at the left and write to the right?

Capital Letters

☐ Did you begin every sentence and name with a capital letter?

End Marks

☐ Do all sentences have end marks?

Spelling

☐ Did you spell your words correctly?

Share

☐ Copy your story neatly onto a clean sheet of paper.

☐ Draw a picture of your story.

☐ Make a puppet of your character.

NARRATIVE WRITING

UNIT 7 Keep Trying • **Lesson 7** *The Hare and The Tortoise*

▶Make-Believe Story

 **Plan**

Who is going to read your make-believe story?

☐ your class

☐ a teacher

☐ a parent

☐ a friend

☐ other _____

- - - - - - - - - - - - - - - - - - -

Why are you writing this story?

☐ to tell about something that can't really happen

☐ to entertain

_____

- - - - - - - - - - - - - - - - - - -

☐ other _____

_____

- - - - - - - - - - - - - - - - - - -

_____

Make-Believe Story • **Writer's Workbook**

Objective: Students make a plan for writing a make-believe story.

Name _____ Date _____

▶**Make-Believe Story**

 **Plan**

Use the story map to plan your
make-believe story.

Characters	Beginning

Middle	End

 **Write**

Use your story map to write a
make-believe story.

NARRATIVE WRITING

▶**Make-Believe Story**

Revise

Read your sentences. Use the checklist to make your make-believe story better. Use these marks to make changes.

Proofreading Marks

∧	Add something.
—	Take out something.
≡	Make a capital letter.
⊙	Add a period.

Ideas

☐ Is it clear that your story is make-believe?

☐ Do you tell enough about what your character does?

☐ Did you write a title for your story?

Order

☐ Does your story have a beginning, middle, and end?

☐ Did you write what happened in an order that makes sense?

Word Choice

☐ Do you tell words that your character says?

Sentence Fluency

☐ Did you write complete sentences?

▶ **Make-Believe Story**

Check

Use this list to help you remember to check everything.

Spacing

☐ Are there spaces between your words and sentences?

Punctuation

☐ Did you write quotation marks at the beginning and end of words that your character said?

Capital Letters

☐ Did you begin every sentence and name with a capital letter?

Spelling

☐ Did you spell your words correctly?

Share

☐ Copy your story neatly onto a clean sheet of paper.

☐ Draw a picture of your story.

☐ Read your story aloud.

NARRATIVE WRITING

UNIT 8 Games • **Lesson 2** *A Game Called Piggle*

▶ Describing an Object

〔 Plan 〕

Who is going to read your writing?

☐ your teacher

☐ your parent

☐ a friend

_____

- -

☐ other _____

Why are you writing a description?

☐ to describe an object used in a game

☐ to describe an object used in a sport

_____

- -

☐ other _____

Write the name of the object you are going to describe.

_____

- -

_____

▶**Describing an Object**

DESCRIPTIVE WRITING

Plan

Use the web to plan your writing.
Write the name of the object in the
middle circle. Then write one idea in
each of the other circles.

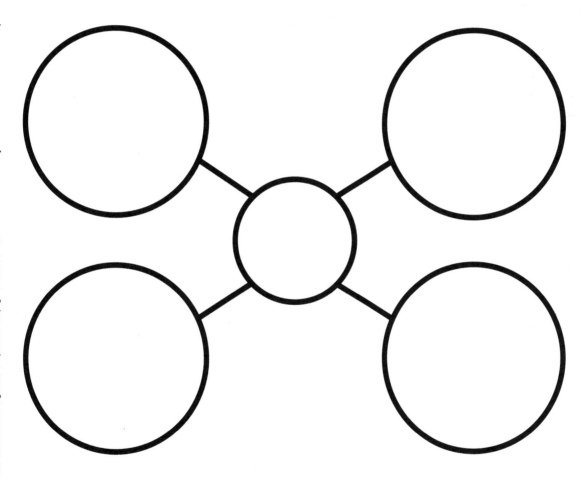

Write

Write your description on a sheet
of paper.

UNIT 8 Games • **Lesson 3** *Jafta*

▶**Describing an Object**

Revise

Use this checklist to make your sentences better. Use proofreading marks to make changes.

Proofreading Marks	
∧	Add something.
—	Take out something.
≡	Make a capital letter.
⊙	Add a period.

Ideas

☐ Did you write about all of the ideas in your web?

☐ Do you want to add details to describe the object?

Organization

☐ Would your sentences make more sense in another order?

☐ Does each sentence tell something different about the object?

Word Choice

☐ Did you use words that describe?

☐ Are there other words you could use to describe the object?

Sentence Fluency

☐ Do the sentences go together?

Objective: Students make a plan and draft a description of an object.

Copyright © SRA/McGraw-Hill. Permission is granted to reproduce this page for classroom use.

▶**Describing an Object**

Check

Use this list to make sure you remember to check everything.

Capital Letters

☐ Did you begin every sentence with a capital letter?

End Marks

☐ Did you write an end mark for every sentence?

Spelling

☐ Did you spell your words correctly?

Share

☐ Copy your writing neatly onto a clean sheet of paper. Use your best handwriting.

☐ Draw a picture of the object you described in your writing.

☐ Read your description aloud to the class.

DESCRIPTIVE WRITING

UNIT 8 Games • **Lesson 5** *Matthew and Tilly*

Objective: Students make a plan for writing a description of a person.

▶Describing a Person

Plan

Who is going to read your writing?

☐ your teacher

☐ your parent

☐ another student

☐ the person you are describing

_____

– –

☐ other _____

Why are you writing this description?

☐ to describe a player in a game

☐ to describe a player in a sport

_____

– –

☐ other _____

Write the name of the person you are going to describe in your writing.

_____

– –

_____

Copyright © SRA/McGraw-Hill. Permission is granted to reproduce this page for classroom use.

▶**Describing a Person**

Plan

Use the web to plan your writing.
Write the person's name in the middle
circle. Then write one idea in each of
the other circles.

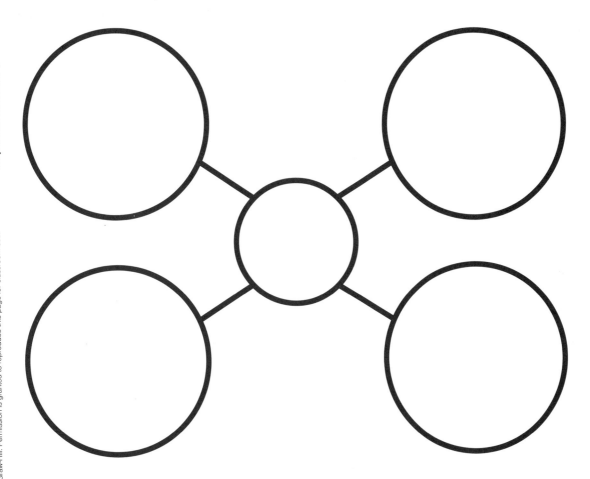

DESCRIPTIVE WRITING

Write

Write your description on a sheet of paper.

▶**Describing a Person**

Objective: Students revise writing by adding, deleting, rearranging, or changing.

Revise

Use this checklist to make your sentences better.

Ideas

☐ Did you write about all of the ideas in your web?

☐ Do you want to add more details to describe the person?

☐ Does each sentence tell something different about the person?

Organization

☐ Would your sentences make more sense in another order?

Word Choice

☐ Did you use words that describe how the person looks and sounds?

☐ Are there other words you could add to your sentences?

Sentence Fluency

☐ Do the sentences go together?

Proofreading Marks

∧	Add something.
—	Take out something.
≡	Make a capital letter.
⊙	Add a period.

▶**Describing a Person**

DESCRIPTIVE WRITING

Check

Use this list to make sure you remember to check everything.

Capital Letters

☐ Did you begin every sentence with a capital letter?

☐ Did you begin the name of the person with a capital letter?

End Marks

☐ Did you write an end mark for every sentence?

Spelling

☐ Did you spell your words correctly?

Share

☐ Copy your writing neatly onto a clean sheet of paper.

☐ Draw a picture of the person you described in your writing.

☐ Trade your writing with a classmate. Read each other's description.

▶Describing an Animal

Plan

Who is going to read your writing?

☐ your parent

☐ your teacher

☐ your grandparent

☐ a friend

_____

☐ other _____

Why are you writing this description?

☐ to describe an animal

_____

☐ other _____

Write the name of the animal you are going to describe in your writing.

_____

_____

Describing an Animal • **Writer's Workbook**

Objective: Students make a plan for writing a description of an animal.

UNIT 8 Games • **Lesson 6** *The Great Ball Game*

▶**Describing an Animal**

Objective: Students plan and draft a description of an animal.

Plan

Use a list to plan your writing. Write
the name of the animal at the top of
the list. Then write one detail about
the animal on each line of the list.

_____

_ _ _ _ _ _ _ _ _ _ _ _ _ _ _ _ _ _

_____

_____

_ _ _ _ _ _ _ _ _ _ _ _ _ _ _ _ _ _

_____

_ _ _ _ _ _ _ _ _ _ _ _ _ _ _ _ _ _

_____

_____

_ _ _ _ _ _ _ _ _ _ _ _ _ _ _ _ _ _

_____

_____

_ _ _ _ _ _ _ _ _ _ _ _ _ _ _ _ _ _

_____

Write

Write your sentences to describe an
animal on a sheet of paper.

DESCRIPTIVE WRITING

▶**Describing an Animal**

Revise

Use this checklist to make your sentences better.

Ideas

☐ Did you write all of the items on your list?

☐ Do you want to add more details to describe the animal?

☐ Do you want to take out any ideas?

Organization

☐ Would your sentences make more sense in a different order?

Word Choice

☐ Are there other words you could use to describe the animal?

☐ Did you use words that begin with repeating sounds?

☐ Did you use contractions in your writing?

Proofreading Marks

∧	Add something.
—	Take out something.
≡	Make a capital letter.
⊙	Add a period.

Name _____ Date _____

▶**Describing an Animal**

Check

Use this list to make sure you remember to check everything.

Capital Letters

☐ Did you begin every sentence with a capital letter?

Punctuation

☐ Did you write contractions correctly?

☐ Did you write the correct end mark for every sentence?

Spelling

☐ Did you spell your words correctly?

Share

☐ Copy your writing neatly on a clean sheet of paper.

☐ Draw a picture of the animal that you described in your writing.

☐ Record your writing on a cassette tape.

☐ Play the tape to a classmate.

DESCRIPTIVE WRITING

UNIT 8 Games • **Lesson 7** *The Big Team Relay Race*

▶Describing a Game

Plan

Who is going to read your writing?

☐ your teacher

☐ your parent

☐ your class

☐ a friend

_____

‒ ‒ ‒ ‒ ‒ ‒ ‒ ‒ ‒ ‒ ‒ ‒ ‒ ‒ ‒ ‒ ‒ ‒ ‒

☐ other _____

Why are you writing this description?

☐ to describe a game

☐ to describe a sporting event

_____

‒ ‒ ‒ ‒ ‒ ‒ ‒ ‒ ‒ ‒ ‒ ‒ ‒ ‒ ‒ ‒ ‒ ‒ ‒

☐ other _____

Write the game or sporting event that you are going to describe.

_____

‒ ‒

_____

Objective: Students make a plan for writing a descriptive paragraph.

Copyright © SRA/McGraw-Hill. Permission is granted to reproduce this page for classroom use.

▶**Describing a Game**

DESCRIPTIVE WRITING

Plan

Use the **web** to plan your paragraph.
Write the name of the game or
sporting event in the middle circle.
Then write one detail in each of the
other circles.

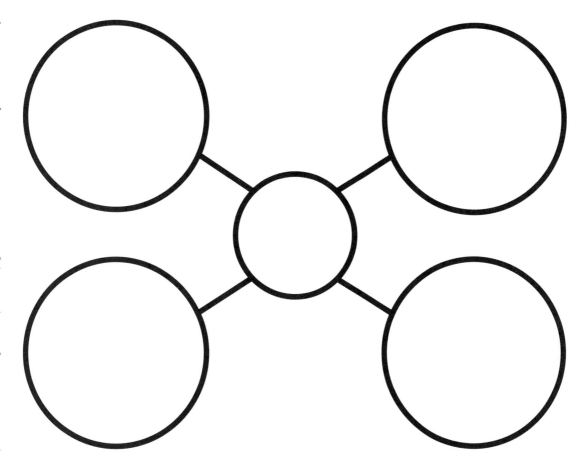

Write

Write your description of a game or
sporting event on a sheet of paper.

▶ **Describing a Game**

Objective: Students revise their writing by adding, deleting, rearranging, or changing.

Revise

Use this checklist to make your sentences better.

Ideas

☐ Do you have enough details about the game or sporting event?

☐ Did you write all the ideas in your web?

☐ Do you want to take out any ideas?

☐ Does each sentence tell about the game or sporting event?

Organization

☐ Did you write a topic sentence?

☐ Do your sentences tell about your topic?

Word Choice

☐ Are there other describing words you could add to your sentences?

Sentence Fluency

☐ Are there any sentences you can take out?

Proofreading Marks

$\wedge$	Add something.
___	Take out something.
$\equiv$	Make a capital letter.
$\odot$	Add a period.

►**Describing a Game**

Check

Use this list to make sure you remember to check everything.

☐ Did you write a title?

☐ Did you leave spaces between your words and sentences?

Capital Letters

☐ Do sentences begin with a capital letter?

End Marks

☐ Did you write the correct end mark for every sentence?

Spelling

☐ Did you spell your words correctly?

Share

☐ Copy your writing neatly onto a clean sheet of paper.

☐ Draw a picture to show what happened in your writing. Put your writing in a book.

DESCRIPTIVE WRITING

Objective: Students generate ideas for a rhyming poem.

▶Rhyming Poem

Plan

Who is going to read your poem?

☐ your teacher

☐ your family

☐ your class

☐ a friend

_____

- -

☐ other _____

Why are you writing a rhyming poem?

☐ to tell about something that scares me

☐ to tell why I am afraid of something

_____

- -

☐ other _____

_____

- -

_____

Copyright © SRA/McGraw-Hill. Permission is granted to reproduce this page for classroom use.

▶Rhyming Poem

POETRY

Plan

Plan your rhyming poem. Write what you are afraid of on the top line. Then write ideas about what you want to say about it on the list.

_____

_ _ _ _ _ _ _ _ _ _ _ _ _ _ _ _ _ _ _

_____

_ _ _ _ _ _ _ _ _ _ _ _ _ _ _ _ _ _ _

_____

_ _ _ _ _ _ _ _ _ _ _ _ _ _ _ _ _ _ _

_____

_ _ _ _ _ _ _ _ _ _ _ _ _ _ _ _ _ _ _

_____

_ _ _ _ _ _ _ _ _ _ _ _ _ _ _ _ _ _ _

Write

Write your rhyming poem on a sheet of paper.

▶**Rhyming Poem**

Objective: Students revise their writing by adding, deleting, rearranging, or changing.

Revise

Read your poem. Use this checklist to make your poem better. Use proofreading marks to make changes.

Proofreading Marks

∧	Add something.
—	Take out something.
≡	Make a capital letter.
⊙	Add a period.

Ideas

☐ Do you tell enough about what makes you afraid?

Organization

☐ Would the lines in your poem make more sense in a different order?

Word Choice

☐ Did you use words that rhyme at the end of each line?

☐ Are there other describing words you could use?

Make all your changes to your poem.

UNIT 9 Being Afraid • **Lesson 2** *My Brother Is Afraid of Just About Everything*

▶**Rhyming Poem**

Check

Use this list to make sure you remember to check everything.

☐ Did you write a title?

☐ Did you spell your words correctly?

☐ Did you put spaces between words?

☐ Does your writing start at the top and go to the bottom?

POETRY

Share

Use the checklist to get your rhyming poem ready to share.

☐ Copy your poem neatly onto a clean sheet of paper. Use your best handwriting.

☐ Draw a picture to go with your poem.

☐ Trade papers with a classmate. Read each other's rhyming poems.

☐ Tell your classmate what you think about the poem.

▶Rhyming Poem

Objective: Students generate ideas for a rhyming poem.

Plan

Who is going to read your poem?

☐ your teacher

☐ your family

☐ your class

☐ a friend

_____

- -

☐ other _____

Why are you writing this poem?

☐ to tell about something that scared me

☐ to tell about something I'm not afraid
  of anymore

_____

- -

☐ other _____

_____

- -

_____

▶**Rhyming Poem**

POETRY

Plan

Use the web to plan your poem. Write what you were afraid of in the middle circle. Then write ideas that tell about it in the outer circles.

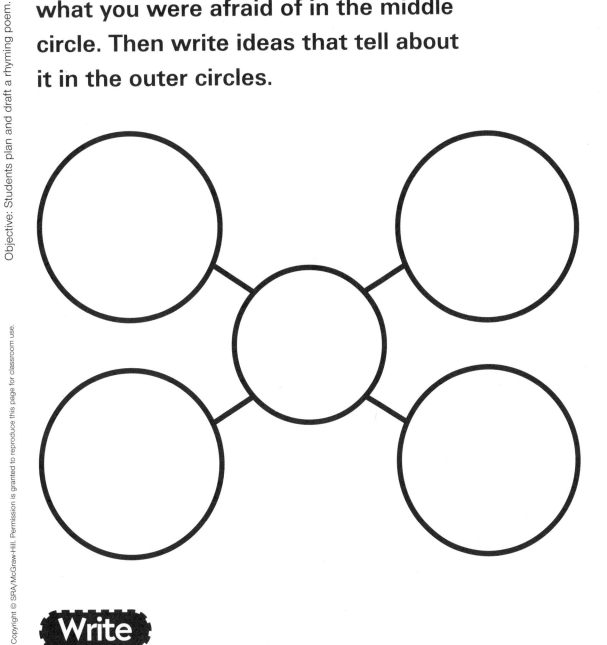

Write

Write your poem on a sheet of paper.

▶**Rhyming Poem**

Revise

Use this checklist to make your poem better. Use proofreading marks to make changes.

Ideas

☐ Do you tell enough to describe your fear?

☐ Do you tell how you found out you did not need to be afraid?

Organization

☐ Does your poem have four lines?

☐ Would the lines in your poem make more sense in a different order?

Word Choice

☐ Do lines one and three rhyme?

☐ Do lines two and four rhyme?

☐ Are there other words you could use?

Make all your changes to your poem.

Proofreading Marks	
∧	Add something.
—	Take out something.
≡	Make a capital letter.
⊙	Add a period.

▶**Rhyming Poem**

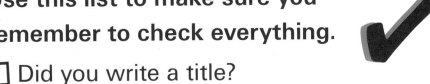

Check

Use this list to make sure you remember to check everything.

☐ Did you write a title?

☐ Did you write capital letters where they belong?

☐ Did you write an end mark at the end of the poem?

☐ Did you spell your words correctly?

POETRY

Share

Use the checklist to get your poem ready to share.

☐ Copy your poem neatly onto a clean sheet of paper.

☐ Draw a picture.

☐ Glue your writing and picture to a large plain sheet of paper.

☐ Draw a patterned border around the edge of the plain paper.

☐ Display your paper on a bulletin board.

UNIT 9 Being Afraid • **Lesson 5** *Strange Bumps*

▶Cinquain

Plan

Who is going to read your poem?

☐ your teacher

☐ your family

☐ your brother or sister

☐ your class

_____

- - - - - - - - - - - - - - - - - - - -

☐ other _____

Why are you writing this poem?

☐ to tell about a scary creature

_____

- - - - - - - - - - - - - - - - - - - -

☐ other _____

Write the idea you will use to write your poem.

_____

- - - - - - - - - - - - - - - - - - - -

_____

Objective: Students generate ideas for a nonrhyming poem.

Cinquain • **Writer's Workbook**

 **Cinquain**

POETRY

Plan

Write the name or kind of creature on the top line. Write ideas to describe, show action, and tell how you feel about it. Write a word for the title.

_____

- -

_____

- -

_____

- -

_____

- -

_____

- -

_____

Write

Write your cinquain poem on a sheet of paper.

Objective: Students revise their writing by adding, deleting, rearranging, or changing.

▶**Cinquain**

Revise

Use this checklist to make your poem better. Use proofreading marks to make changes.

Ideas

☐ Did you write about a scary creature?

☐ Did you tell how the creature looks?

☐ Did you tell what the creature does?

Organization

☐ Does your poem have five lines?

☐ Did you write the correct number of words in each line?

Word Choice

☐ Did you use the correct kinds of words in each line?

Make changes to your cinquain.

Proofreading Marks	
∧	Add something.
—	Take out something.
≡	Make a capital letter.
⊙	Add a period.

▶**Cinquain**

POETRY

Check

Use this list to make sure you remember to check everything.

☐ Did you begin names with and write **I** as a capital letter?

☐ Did you put an end mark after each sentence?

☐ Did you write a comma between words in a series?

☐ Did you spell your words correctly?

Share

Use the checklist to get your cinquain poem ready to share.

☐ Copy your cinquain neatly on a clean sheet of paper. Use your best handwriting.

☐ Make a puppet of your scary creature.

☐ Display your poem and puppet in the classroom library. Your classmates can use your puppet when they read your poem.

▶Word Poem

Plan

Who is going to read your word poem?

☐ a parent

☐ your teacher

☐ your grandparent

☐ a friend

☐ other _____

Why are you writing this poem?

☐ to write about a person

☐ to write about an animal

☐ to write about an object

☐ other _____

Write the idea you will use to write a word poem.

_____

_____

_____

▶ **Word Poem**

POETRY

Plan

Write your topic on the top line for the title. Then write one word that begins with each letter in your title.

_____

- -

_____

_____

- -

_____

- -

_____

- -

_____

- -

_____

Write

Write your word poem on a sheet of paper.

▶**Word Poem**

Revise

Use this checklist to make your word poem better. Use proofreading marks to make changes.

Ideas

☐ Did you use words that tell about your topic?

☐ Did you write one word for each letter in the title word?

Organization

☐ Did you write the letters to spell the title word down the paper?

Word Choice

☐ Do words start with the correct letters?

☐ Are there other words you could use?

Make changes to your word poem.

Proofreading Marks

∧	Add something.
—	Take out something.
≡	Make a capital letter.
⊙	Add a period.

Objective: Students revise their writing by adding, deleting, rearranging, or changing.

Copyright © SRA/McGraw

Permission is granted to reproduce this page for classroom use.

▶**Word Poem**

Check

Use this list to make sure you remember to check everything.

☐ Did you spell your title word correctly?

☐ Did you spell your words correctly?

☐ Did you use capital letters for your title word?

Share

Use the checklist to get your word poem ready to share.

☐ Copy your word poem neatly on a clean sheet of paper. Use your best handwriting.

☐ Draw a picture of yourself and the topic of your word poem.

☐ Read your word poem aloud to a classmate.

☐ Place your picture and poem in a class book.

POETRY

Objective: Students generate ideas for a pattern poem.

Copyright © SRA/McGraw-Hill. Permission is granted to reproduce this page for classroom use.

▶ Pattern Poem

Plan

Who is going to read your pattern poem?

☐ your teacher

☐ your family

☐ your class

☐ the person in your poem

_____

– – – – – – – – – – – – – – – – – – –

☐ other _____

Why are you writing this poem?

☐ to tell about a person

_____

– – – – – – – – – – – – – – – – – – –

☐ other _____

Write the idea you will use to write your pattern poem.

I am going to write a pattern poem about

_____

– – – – – – – – – – – – – – – – – – –

UNIT 9 Being Afraid • **Lesson 10** *The Three Billy Goats Gruff*

▶ **Pattern Poem**

Use a list to help plan your pattern poem.
Write the person's name at the top of
the list. Then write four words that you
will use to tell about the person in your
poem. Make three words rhyme.

_____

- -

_____

_____

- -

_____

- -

_____

_____

- -

_____

_____

- -

_____

**Write your pattern poem on a sheet
of paper.**

Objective: Students revise their writing by adding, deleting, rearranging, or changing.

▶ **Pattern Poem**

Revise

Use this checklist to make your pattern poem better. Use proofreading marks to make changes.

Proofreading Marks

$\wedge$	Add something.
——	Take out something.
$\equiv$	Make a capital letter.
$\odot$	Add a period.

Ideas

☐ Did you use words that tell about your topic?

Organization

☐ Did you write four lines?

☐ Does your poem follow the rhythm pattern?

Word Choice

☐ Did you write rhyming words at the end of lines one, two, and four?

☐ Are there other words you could use?

Make changes to your pattern poem.

▶**Pattern Poem**

POETRY

Check

Use this list to make sure you remember to check everything.

☐ Did you write a title?

☐ Did you write a capital letter at the beginning of every name and line?

☐ Did you write an end mark at the end of the poem?

☐ Did you spell your words correctly?

Share

Use the checklist to get your pattern poem ready to share.

☐ Copy your pattern poem neatly onto a clean sheet of paper. Use your best handwriting.

☐ Draw a picture of the person in your poem.

☐ Read your poem to a small group. Have the group clap the rhythm as you read your poem.

☐ Record your poem.

▶ Making a Poster

Plan

Who is going to see your poster?

☐ your school

☐ your class

☐ your neighborhood

☐ your family

☐ your town

_____

☐ other _____

Why are you making this poster?

☐ to tell about different kinds of homes

☐ to tell about the best kind of home
   for a certain place

_____

☐ other _____

_____

_____

Name _____ Date _____

▶**Making a Poster**

PERSUASIVE WRITING

Plan

Draw a picture of the land area.

Write the kind of land on the top line.

Then write a list of the kinds of homes

that would be good in this place.

_____

– –

_____

_____

– –

_____

_____

– –

_____

Write

Write your sentence. Draw a picture

of the house in the place where it

belongs.

▶**Making a Poster**

Revise

Look at your picture. Use this checklist to make your poster better. Use proofreading marks to make changes in your sentence.

Proofreading Marks	
∧	Add something.
—	Take out something.
≡	Make a capital letter.
⊙	Add a period.

Ideas

☐ Does your picture tell about the area where the house is?

☐ Does your sentence tell why this house is the best kind of house?

☐ Do you want to add anything to your sentence or picture?

Organization

☐ Would your sentence look better in another part of the poster?

Word Choice

☐ Are there other words you could use to tell why this kind of house is best?

☐ Are there other words you could use to tell about the place?

Objective: Students revise their writing by adding, deleting, rearranging, or changing.

▶**Making a Poster**

PERSUASIVE WRITING

Check

Neat writing and a colorful picture will make people look at your poster. Use this list to make sure you remember to check everything.

☐ Did you leave space between your words?

☐ Does your writing go from left to right?

☐ Did you begin your sentence with a capital letter?

☐ Did you write an end mark after your sentence?

☐ Did you spell your words correctly?

Share

☐ Draw and color your picture on a clean sheet of drawing paper.

☐ Paste your picture to a piece of poster board.

☐ Write your sentence below your picture. Use your best handwriting.

UNIT 10 Homes • **Lesson 4** *A House Is a House For Me*

▶**Making a Poster**

Who is going to see your poster?

☐ people who live far away

☐ your family

☐ your class

☐ people in your town

_____

– – – – – – – – – – – – – – – – – – – –

☐ other _____

Why are you making this poster?

☐ to tell people how nice your town is

☐ to tell people why they should live in
your town

_____

– – – – – – – – – – – – – – – – – – – –

☐ other _____

Write the idea you will use.

_____

– – – – – – – – – – – – – – – – – – – –

Objective: Students generate ideas for a poster.

Copyright © SRA/McGraw-Hill. Permission is granted to reproduce this page for classroom use.

 Homes • **Lesson 4** *A House Is a House For Me*

▶ **Making a Poster**

PERSUASIVE WRITING

Plan

Write the name of your town. Then write why you like living in your town. Draw a picture to go with each idea.

_____

- - - - - - - - - - - - - - - - -

_____

_____

- - - - - - - - - - - - - - - - -

_____

_____

- - - - - - - - - - - - - - - - -

_____

Write

Draw a picture and write words for your poster on a sheet of paper.

Objective: Students revise their writing by adding, deleting, rearranging, or changing.

► **Making a Poster**

Revise

Read the writing on your poster. Use this checklist to make your poster better. Use proofreading marks to make changes.

Proofreading Marks

∧	Add something.
—	Take out something.
≡	Make a capital letter.
⊙	Add a period.

Ideas

☐ Do your words tell what is best about your town?

☐ Does your picture show what your words tell?

Organization

☐ Could your picture and sentence or words be placed in a different way on your poster?

Word Choice

☐ Did you write the exact words you wanted?

☐ Are there other words you could use?

Make your changes on your sheet of paper.

UNIT 10 Homes • **Lesson 4** *A House Is a House For Me*

▶**Making a Poster**

Check

Your poster should make the reader think and feel a special way. Use this list to make sure you remember to check everything.

☐ Did you spell your words correctly?

☐ Did you begin your sentence with a capital letter?

☐ Did you write an end mark after your sentence?

Share

Use the checklist to get your poster ready to share.

☐ Draw and color your picture.

☐ Paste your picture on poster board.

☐ Write your sentence or words neatly on the poster. Use your best handwriting.

☐ Display your poster in your school's hallways or library.

PERSUASIVE WRITING

Objective: Students generate ideas for writing an advertisement.

UNIT 10 Homes • **Lesson 5** *Animal Homes*

►Advertisement

Plan

Who is going to see your advertisement?

☐ your teacher

☐ your parent

☐ a pet owner

☐ a pet store owner

☐ a friend

_____

– – – – – – – – – – – – – – – – – –

☐ other _____

Why are you writing an advertisement?

☐ to tell about a new kind of pet shelter

☐ to make someone think your pet
home is a good idea

_____

– – – – – – – – – – – – – – – – – –

☐ other _____

_____

– – – – – – – – – – – – – – – – – –

_____

Copyright © SRA/McGraw-Hill. Permission is granted to reproduce this page for classroom use.

Advertisement • Writer's Workbook

 **UNIT 10** Homes • **Lesson 5** *Animal Homes*

▶**Advertisement**

Objective: Students make a plan and draft an advertisement.

Plan

Use the web to plan your advertisement.
Write your idea about the new kind of
pet home in the middle circle. Write
reasons why your pet home would be
a good idea in the outer circles.

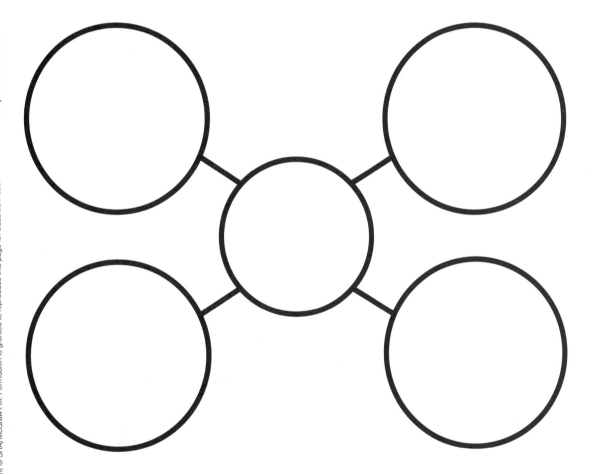

Write

Write your advertisement on a sheet
of paper.

PERSUASIVE WRITING

Objective: Students revise their writing by adding, deleting, rearranging, or changing.

▶**Advertisement**

Revise

Use this checklist to make your advertisement better.

Ideas

☐ Do your words and pictures tell about the pet home?

☐ Do your words and pictures show that it is a good idea?

☐ Did you write all the reasons you wanted to tell?

☐ Do your words and pictures go together?

Organization

☐ Would your words or pictures make more sense and be clearer in a different order?

Word Choice

☐ Did you write words that describe?

☐ Are there other words you could use?

Make any changes to your advertisement.

Proofreading Marks

∧	Add something.
—	Take out something.
≡	Make a capital letter.
⊙	Add a period.

Copyright © SRA/McGraw-Hill. Permission is granted to reproduce this page for classroom use.

▶ **Advertisement**

Check

Your advertisement should be easy to understand. Use this list to make sure you remember to check everything.

☐ Did you spell your words correctly?

☐ Did you write a capital letter at the beginning of your sentence?

☐ Did you write an end mark after your sentence?

Share

Use the checklist to get your advertisement ready to share.

☐ Draw and color your picture on a large sheet of paper.

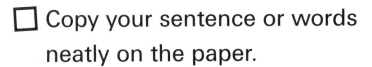

☐ Copy your sentence or words neatly on the paper.

☐ Display your advertisement in your classroom.

☐ Put your advertisement in a class collection.

PERSUASIVE WRITING

▶ Writing a Letter

Plan

Who is going to read your letter?

☐ your teacher

☐ the groundhog in the story

☐ a classmate

_____

☐ other _____

Why are you writing a letter?

☐ to make the groundhog want to share
its home with the bunny

_____

☐ other _____

Write your idea for a letter.

I will write a letter to

_____

_____

▶ **Writing a Letter**

Think about what you want to say in your letter. Write your ideas in order below.

First

Next

Last

Write

Write your letter on a sheet of paper.

Objective: Students plan and draft a persuasive letter.

Copyright © SRA/McGraw-Hill. Permission is granted to reproduce this page for classroom use.

PERSUASIVE WRITING

Name _____ Date _____

▶**Writing a Letter**

Objective: Students revise their writing by adding, deleting, rearranging, or changing.

Revise

Use this checklist to make your letter better.

Ideas

☐ Did you try to make the reader think or feel a certain way?

☐ Does your letter tell all of your reasons?

Organization

☐ Did you write the date, a greeting, and a closing?

☐ Are your sentences in an order that makes sense?

Word Choice

☐ Are there words you could change to make your reasons stronger?

☐ Are there words you could add to tell more?

Sentence Fluency

☐ Does each sentence tell a different reason?

Proofreading Marks

∧	Add something.
—	Take out something.
≡	Make a capital letter.
⊙	Add a period.

▶ **Writing a Letter**

Check

Use this list to make sure you remember to check everything.

☐ Did you begin the name of the month with a capital letter?

☐ Did you begin names and sentences with a capital letter?

☐ Did you write an end mark after every sentence?

☐ Did you spell your words correctly?

Share

☐ Copy your letter neatly onto a clean sheet of paper.

☐ Address an envelope. Then check the envelope.

☐ Put your letter in the envelope. Draw a stamp on the envelope.

☐ Mail your letter in the classroom mailbox.

☐ Pick a letter out of the mailbox. Read it.

PERSUASIVE WRITING

Name _____ Date _____

▶Writing a Paragraph

Who is going to read your paragraph?

☐ your parent

☐ your grandparent

☐ your teacher

☐ your principal

☐ your neighbor

_____

☐ other _____

Why are you writing this paragraph?

☐ to try to make someone let me do something I want to do

☐ to try to make someone take me somewhere I want to go

☐ to try to make someone buy something I want

_____

☐ other _____

Writing a Paragraph • **Writer's Workbook**

Objective: Students generate ideas for a persuasive paragraph.

Copyright © SRA/McGraw-Hill. Permission is granted to reproduce this page for classroom use.

UNIT 10   Homes • **Lesson 9** *The Three Little Pigs*

▶ **Writing a Paragraph**

P E R S U A S I V E   W R I T I N G

Plan

Use the web to plan your paragraph. Write what you want the person to do in the middle circle. Write a different reason telling why this is a good idea in each of the outer circles.

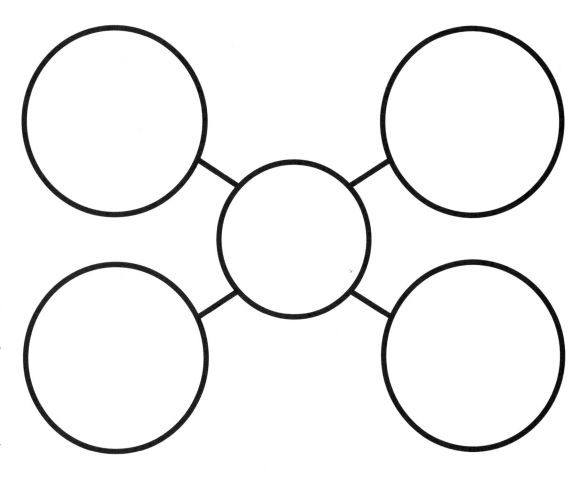

Write

Write your paragraph on a sheet of paper.

▶ **Writing a Paragraph**

Objective: Students revise their writing by adding, deleting, rearranging, or changing.

Revise

Use this checklist to make your paragraph better.

Proofreading Marks

∧	Add something.
—	Take out something.
≡	Make a capital letter.
⊙	Add a period.

Ideas

☐ Did you tell the reader exactly what you want?

☐ Did you write your best reasons?

☐ Do you have enough reasons to help make the reader agree with you?

Organization

☐ Did you tell what you want in the first sentence?

☐ Would your sentences make more sense in another order?

Word Choice

☐ Are there other words you could use to make your reasons better?

Sentence Fluency

☐ Does each sentence lead to the next one?

UNIT 10   Homes • **Lesson 10** *Unit Wrap-Up*

▶**Writing a Paragraph**

PERSUASIVE WRITING

Check

Use this list to make sure you remember to check everything.

☐ Did you write capital letters where they belong in the title?

☐ Did you begin every sentence with a capital letter?

☐ Did you use a capital letter to write the word I?

☐ Did you write an end mark after every sentence?

☐ Did you spell your words correctly?

Share

☐ Copy your paragraph neatly onto a clean sheet of paper.

☐ Trade papers with a friend. Read each other's paragraphs.

☐ Put your writing and picture in a class book.

☐ Give the book to grown-up visitors to read when they visit your classroom.

▶Cumulative Checklists

Revising

Ideas

☐ Did you say everything you wanted to say?

☐ Do you want to add an idea?

☐ Do you want to take out an idea?

☐ Do your sentences tell enough about the topic?

☐ Do you want to add more details?

☐ Did you tell something that was interesting to your reader?

☐ Did you write a title?

☐ Did you use all the ideas from your plan?

Order/Organization

☐ Would your sentences make more sense in another order?

☐ Did you write a beginning, middle, and end?

☐ Does each sentence tell about the topic?

☐ Does each sentence tell something new?

Revising

Word Choice

- [ ] Are there other words you can use to make your ideas easy to follow?

- [ ] Are there words you can add to make your sentences more interesting?

- [ ] Are there any other describing words you can use to tell more details?

- [ ] Does each sentence tell exactly what you mean?

- [ ] Do you need to add any words with repeating sounds?

Sentence Fluency

- [ ] Did you write complete sentences?

- [ ] Do your sentences go together?

REVISING CHECKLIST

Check

- ☐ Spelling
- ☐ Spaces between Words
- ☐ Writing from Left to Right
- ☐ Writing from Top to Bottom

Unit 1 Mechanics

Lessons 1–3 ☐ Capital Letters: Names of People and the Word *I*

Lessons 6–8 ☐ Capital Letters: Cities and States

Lessons 11–13 ☐ Sentences: Capital Letters and Periods

Unit 2 Grammar and Usage

Lessons 1–3 ☐ Adjectives

Lessons 6–8 ☐ Types of Sentences

Unit 3 Grammar and Usage

Lessons 1–3 ☐ Possessive Nouns

Lessons 6–8 ☐ Singular and Plural Nouns

REVISING CHECKLIST

Unit 4 Mechanics

Lessons 1–3 ☐ Capitalization: Days and Months

Lessons 6–8 ☐ End Punctuation

Unit 5 Grammar and Usage

Lessons 1–3 ☐ Adjectives

Lessons 6–8 ☐ Verbs

Unit 6 Mechanics

Lessons 1–3 ☐ Commas in a Series

Lessons 6–8 ☐ Capitalization: Cities and States

Unit 7 Grammar and Usage

Lessons 1–2 ☐ Past Tense Verbs

Lesson 3 ☐ Pronouns

Lesson 4 ☐ Possessive Pronouns

Lesson 5 ☐ Adjectives That Compare

Unit 8 Grammar and Usage

Lessons 1–2 ☐ Kinds of Sentences

Lessons 4–5 ☐ Sentence Parts

Lesson 6 ☐ Contractions

Share

Get your writing ready to share.

☐ Copy your work onto a clean sheet of paper. Use your best handwriting.

☐ Draw a picture to go with your writing.

☐ Label your picture.

Share your writing.

☐ Read your writing aloud to your class. Ask your classmates what they think of your writing.

☐ Give your writing to someone else, such as a family member.

☐ Trade your writing with a classmate.

☐ Post your writing on the class bulletin board or in the school hallway.

☐ Put your poem into a class book.

Share

- ☐ Turn your own writing into a book by making a front and back cover.

- ☐ Put your writing in your classroom library.

- ☐ Put your writing in the school library or media center.

- ☐ Make a puppet of a character. Use the puppet to tell the story. Put your puppet and story in your classroom library. Your classmates can use the puppet when they read your story later.

- ☐ Record your writing onto a cassette tape, and play it for the class.

- ☐ Make a poster from your writing. Glue your writing onto poster board or a large piece of paper. Decorate the poster.

- ☐ If you have written a poem, read it to a small group. Have the group clap the rhythm after you read each line.

SHARING CHECKLIST